rTip

T0011499

Disappearing Ice Sheets

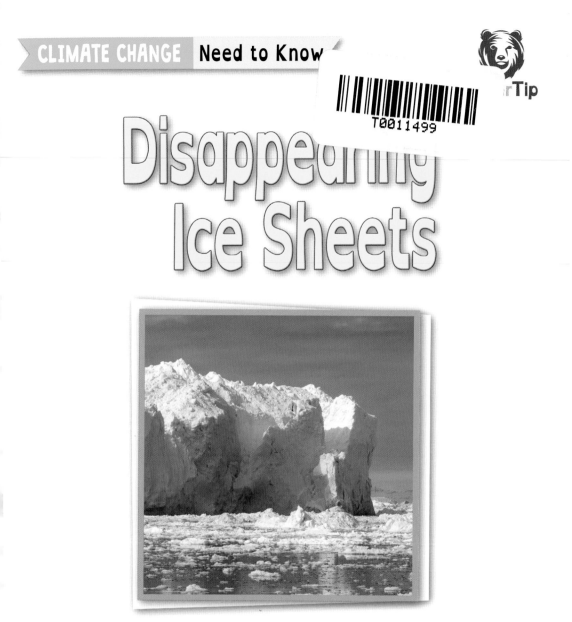

by Ashley Kuehl

Consultant: Jordan Stoleru, Science Educator

BEARPORT
PUBLISHING

Minneapolis, Minnesota

Credits

Cover and title page, © Anders Peter Photography/Shutterstock; 4–5, © Robert Marxen/ Shutterstock; 7T, © Wojciech Dziadosz/Shutterstock; 7B, © Tobetv/Shutterstock; 9, © Maridav/ Shutterstock; 10–11, © Georgii Shipin/Shutterstock; 13, © Panksvatouny/Shutterstock; 14–15, © Olga Gavrilova/Shutterstock; 17, © Jorn Pilon/Shutterstock; 18–19, © kasakphoto/Shutterstock; 21, © Peter Gudella/Shutterstock; 22–23, © Sasha Samardzija/Shutterstock; 25, © FotoKina/Shutterstock; 27, © FatCamera/iStock; 28, © Pyty/Shutterstock.

Bearport Publishing Company Product Development Team

President: Jen Jenson; Director of Product Development: Spencer Brinker; Managing Editor: Allison Juda; Associate Editor: Naomi Reich; Associate Editor: Tiana Tran; Art Director: Colin O'Dea; Designer: Elena Klinkner; Designer: Kayla Eggert; Product Development Assistant: Owen Hamlin

STATEMENT ON USAGE OF GENERATIVE ARTIFICIAL INTELLIGENCE
Bearport Publishing remains committed to publishing high-quality nonfiction books. Therefore, we restrict the use of generative AI to ensure accuracy of all text and visual components pertaining to a book's subject. See BearportPublishing.com for details.

Library of Congress Cataloging-in-Publication Data is available at www.loc.gov or upon request from the publisher.

ISBN: 979-8-88916-525-5 (hardcover)
ISBN: 979-8-88916-532-3 (paperback)
ISBN: 979-8-88916-538-5 (ebook)

For more information, write to Bearport Publishing, 5357 Penn Avenue South, Minneapolis, MN 55419.

Contents

Ancient Ice

More than 30 million years ago, **glaciers** began forming in Antarctica. The giant pieces of ice grew larger and larger. Over time, a sheet of ice stretched out to cover millions of miles.

But something has changed. Antarctic ice is now disappearing. What is happening?

Glaciers don't stay in one place. They move across land. Most parts of Antarctica's ice travel very slowly.

Sheets of Ice

Glaciers are big chunks of ice that form on land. Some are huge. Large glaciers that spread out in all directions are called **ice sheets**. Earth has two ice sheets. One covers most of Antarctica. Another has formed over much of Greenland.

There are a few kinds of glaciers. Ice caps are similar to ice sheets but smaller. Ice shelves are parts of glaciers that stick out over the oceans.

Antarctic ice sheet

Greenland ice sheet

Ice sheets melt a little bit during warmer parts of the year. They refreeze when things cool down again. This is part of how they grow and spread. But now ice sheets are melting more than ever before. They are not refreezing as much water. The ice is shrinking.

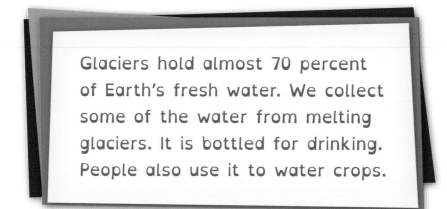

Glaciers hold almost 70 percent of Earth's fresh water. We collect some of the water from melting glaciers. It is bottled for drinking. People also use it to water crops.

Heating Up

One of the major causes of more melting is **climate change.** Earth's patterns of usual weather, or climates, are changing. Many parts of the world are getting hotter. Human activities are a big reason things are heating up.

Weather is what happens at one time. It might be sunny, hot, or windy out. Climate is the usual weather from year to year.

We burn **fossil fuels** to make energy. This powers our homes and businesses. Fossil fuels help make our cars go. But burning fossil fuels lets out **greenhouse gases.** These gases trap heat around the planet. As we add more to the air around Earth, the planet gets hotter and hotter.

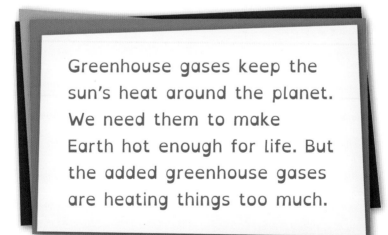

Greenhouse gases keep the sun's heat around the planet. We need them to make Earth hot enough for life. But the added greenhouse gases are heating things too much.

Factories that make the things we need often let out a lot of greenhouse gases.

Melting Ice Sheets

The extra heat is catching up with Earth's ice. In the past 30 years, ice sheets in both Antarctica and Greenland have shrunk. More than 8 trillion tons (7 trillion t) of ice have melted. That's enough to make a cube of ice 12 miles (19 km) high!

Antarctica's ice sheet is melting quickly. But Greenland is losing even more ice every year. About 270 billion tn. (245 billion t) disappear annually.

Losing Earth's Cool

As ice sheets melt, they get thinner. The ice left behind is weaker and breaks more easily. Thin pieces along the edges crack off and make the ice sheets even smaller.

Warmer ocean waters are also a problem. The edges of ice sheets near the water melt more quickly.

Ocean water can hold more heat than land. About 90 percent of the extra heat from climate change has been taken in by the oceans.

Melting ice makes a warming planet worse. White ice **reflects** the sun. This keeps things cooler by bouncing heat away from Earth. When ice melts, the land below shows. The dark-colored land takes in heat. That makes Earth even hotter. More ice melts.

Ice reflects about 90 percent of the sun's light and heat back into space. So, losing ice makes a big impact on Earth's temperature.

Rising Seas

Melting ice sheets send water rushing into the oceans. This extra water makes **sea levels** rise. The water then pushes onto land. Since 1901, sea levels have risen about 8 inches (20 cm). Scientists think they could rise another foot (30 cm) by 2050.

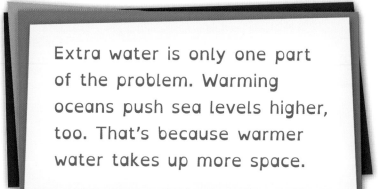

Extra water is only one part of the problem. Warming oceans push sea levels higher, too. That's because warmer water takes up more space.

Flooding is a big concern as sea levels rise. Along the coasts, floods can damage buildings where people work and live. They can harm plant and animal habitats, too. Some low islands may soon disappear under rising water.

Some people who live along the coast are moving. They are going further inland to get away from floods. Others are building walls or putting in plants to help stop floods.

Flood walls stop some water from coming onto land.

Changing Weather

Higher sea levels and warmer water also change the weather worldwide. One major threat is **hurricanes**. Warmer seawater heats the air above it. That causes bigger storms and faster winds. A warmer climate makes those storms happen more often.

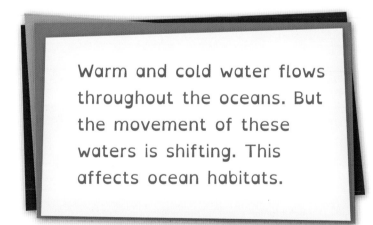

Warm and cold water flows throughout the oceans. But the movement of these waters is shifting. This affects ocean habitats.

How Can We Help?

It's not too late to slow climate change. We can help stop ice sheets from disappearing. If people burned fewer fossil fuels, we would let out fewer greenhouse gases. We can all work together to slow the melt.

If it is safe, walk or ride a bike to get where you need to go. Turn out lights when you leave a room. Unplug electronics you are not using. Little changes can make a big difference.

Antarctica Disappearing

Antarctica has long been covered in an ice sheet. In recent years, the ice has shrunk. The shape of the ice around the continent has changed.

Antarctica's Average Ice

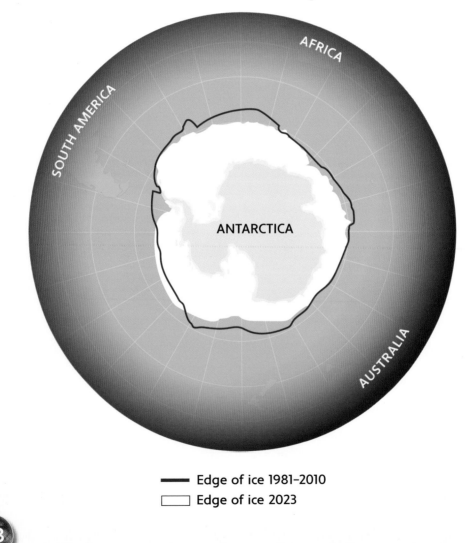

——— Edge of ice 1981–2010

☐ Edge of ice 2023

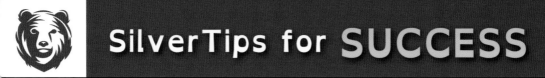
★ SilverTips for REVIEW

Review what you've learned. Use the text to help you.

Define key terms

climate change   ice sheets

fossil fuels   sea levels

greenhouse gases

Check for understanding

What are ice sheets?

Describe why ice sheets are melting and what is making them melt faster.

What problems are caused by melting ice?

Think deeper

Think about where you live. What might happen to your home if ice sheets continue to disappear?

★ SilverTips on TEST-TAKING

- **Make a study plan.** Ask your teacher what the test is going to cover. Then, set aside time to study a little bit every day.

- **Read all the questions carefully.** Be sure you know what is being asked.

- **Skip any questions** you don't know how to answer right away. Mark them and come back later if you have time.

Glossary

climate change changes in the usual weather patterns around Earth, including the warming of the air and oceans, due to human activities

fossil fuels energy sources, such as coal, oil, and gas, made from the remains of plants and animals that died millions of years ago

glaciers large, slow-moving pieces of ice found on land

greenhouse gases gases that trap warm air around Earth

hurricanes powerful storms with heavy rain and fast winds that form over large bodies of water

ice sheets large glaciers that spread out over land in all directions

reflects bounces back

sea levels the average height of the oceans' surface

Read More

Bergin, Raymond. *Melting Ice (What on Earth? Climate Change Explained).* Minneapolis: Bearport Publishing Company, 2022.

Golkar, Golriz. *Ancient Ice: What Glaciers Reveal about Climate Change.* Mankato, MN: Capstone Press, 2024.

Hill, Christina. *Oceans, Glaciers, and Rising Sea Levels: A Graphic Guide (The Climate Crisis).* Minneapolis: Graphic Universe, 2024.

Learn More Online

1. Go to **www.factsurfer.com** or scan the QR code below.

2. Enter "**Disappearing Ice**" into the search box.

3. Click on the cover of this book to see a list of websites.

Index

About the Author

Ashley Kuehl is an editor and writer specializing in nonfiction for young people. She lives in Minneapolis, MN.